The New Novello Choral Edition

ANTONÍN DVOŘÁK

Requiem

for soprano, alto, tenor and bass soloists, SATB choir and orchestra

Vocal score

Edited by Michael Pilkington

Order No: NOV072516

NOVELLO PUBLISHING LIMITED

Cover illustration: first page of the autograph score of Dvořák's *Requiem* (courtesy of the Muzeum Antonína Dvořáka, Prague).

This new edition of the *Requiem* follows the layout of the previous edition (catalogue number NOV 070088) page for page, to allow this new edition to be used side-by-side with the edition it supersedes.

© 2001 Novello & Company Limited
Published in Great Britain by Novello Publishing Limited - Head Office: 14-15 Berners Street, London W1T 3LJ
Tel +44 (0)20 7434 0066   Fax +44 (0)20 7287 6329
Sales and Hire: Music Sales Distribution Centre – Newmarket Road, Bury St Edmunds, Suffolk IP33 3YB
Tel +44 (0)1284 702600   Fax +44 (0)1284 768301
www.musicsales.com   e-mail: music@musicsales.co.uk
All rights reserved   Printed in Great Britain
Music setting by Stave Origination

Orchestral material is available on hire from the Publisher. It is requested that on all concert notices and programmes acknowledgement is made to 'The New Novello Choral Edition'. Permission to reproduce from the Preface of this Edition must be obtained from the Publisher.

PREFACE

Dvořák began work on his *Requiem* on New Year's Day, 1890, and completed the vocal score on 18 July and the full score on 31 October. The first performance of the work was at the Birmingham Musical Festival on 9 October 1891. Novello published a vocal score for use at this performance, using Dvořák's own completed vocal score, and the following year published the full score. Not surprisingly, in the process of orchestration, Dvořák made a number of changes, some of which reached the Novello vocal score. At the end of the MS vocal score, however, Dvořák has made the following note: 'Here and there I made corrections, but forgot to put them into the proofs, and shall now wait for the Birmingham performance to do so.'[1] In fact the changes are quite considerable, making it essential to create a new piano reduction for this edition.

For the full score, Dvořák provided a fair copy made from his autograph, corrected by him in pencil. This score is now held in the Royal College of Music Library, and I am grateful to the College for allowing me to use it as the basis for this edition. It is clear that the engraver of the Novello full score must have been working in a hurry, and also that he was familiar with the printed vocal score. There are a large number of discrepancies between Dvořák's fair copy and the printed full score, and in most cases where the vocal parts had been revised the printed score follows the vocal score.

In 1955 a complete edition of the works of Dvořák was begun by Czech scholars. In 1960 a vocal score of the *Requiem* was published, and the following year a full score appeared. The basis for this edition was the autograph full score, held by the composer's heirs, and the Novello full score of 1892. Unfortunately, the editors did not have access to the fair copy, held by Novello at that time, and were only able to learn of a few of the differences from an English musicologist, Dr John Clapham of the University of Wales. As a result, the editors state that 'The basis for the present edition is Novello's edition, published in the composer's lifetime and under his supervision.'[1] Where there are differences between the autograph and the Novello edition, they usually follow Novello. In most cases, however, the autograph and the fair copy agree and it is the printed score that is in error.

EDITORIAL PROCEDURE.

The primary source for the present edition is the fair copy of the full score made for Novello and corrected by the composer. The Editors' Notes in the Complete Works full score are extremely detailed, and list most readings in which the autograph differs from the printed score. Where the autograph and the fair copy agree, this edition follows them without further comment. Where they do not agree, or where the Complete Works makes no specific comment, information will be found in the footnotes, or in the Critical Commentary which follows. Dynamic indications in square brackets and slurs and hairpins with strokes are editorial suggestions where markings in the sources appear to be inconsistent or missing.

SOURCES

A   Fair copy of Full Score revised by the composer and provided for Novello's engraver. This is a very clear copy, with a number of corrections by Dvořák in pencil, which include all the MM markings. There are also some markings in blue which may have been made by the engraver - in most cases they adjust the music to that given in **E**.

B   Full Score, 1892, Novello.

C   Complete Works Full Score, edited by Jarmil Burghauser, 1961, Supraphon.

D   Autograph MS of full score, as reported in Editors' Notes to **C**, above. It appears that Dvořák made a few further modifications to this score after **A** had been copied.

E   Vocal Score, 1891, Novello.

F   Complete Works Vocal Score, agreeing with **C** unless otherwise noted; 1960, Supraphon.

CRITICAL NOTES

I

Bars 33-4 Double Bass: These bars are blank in **A** and **B**; according to **C** the notes given were added to **D** at a late stage. They are obviously correct, see Bassoon 2.

Bar 70. A page turn led to the omission of some woodwind notes in **A**. Those given for flutes were added in pencil, followed by **B** and **C**. However, the oboes were given b′♭ as the pencilled correction, in spite of the tie from the f′ on the previous page; **B** has an empty bar and no tie, **C** has f′, probably correct.

Bar 118, Bassoon note 5: e′♮ in **A**, **B** and **D**, c′♯ in **C**, matching cellos; **D** also had e′♮ for cellos before revision.

Bar 147. There is a page turn in **A** and **D**, and horn 2 is left blank in spite of tie from previous bar. **B** has rests, **C** sustains low f to beat 1 of bar 150; the change in dynamics suggests beat 1 of bar 148 an equally possible stopping place.

Bars 149-50, Double Bass: The staccato dots are clearly changed to stress marks in **A**, though they remain staccato in **B** and **C**.

II

Tempo marks vary.

Bar 21: **Meno - Tempo I - Meno mosso**, **D**; nothing in **A** or **B**; **Meno mosso Tempo I**, **C**; **Tempo I**, **E**.

Bar 33: **Un poco più mosso**, **D**; nothing, but **Poco più mosso** added in blue, **A**, and given in **B**, **C** and **E**.

Bar 45: **Meno mosso - tempo I**, **D**; nothing in **A**, **Meno mosso, quasi tempo I**, **B** followed by **C**, **A tempo** in **E**. Incidentally, **B**, **C**, and **E** have a **rit.** in bar 43, though none is given in **A** or **D**.

Bars 66-7, Bassoon 1 (upper part of LH in vocal score): all d′♭s in **A**, **C** and **D**. They were changed in blue pencil (the engraver?) to e′♭s in **A**, and are given as e′♭s in **B**, **E** and **F**; see bars 62-3.

IV

Bars 3, 7, 11, Tam-tam: an open tie is used in this edition as in **C** to replace the pause given in **A**, **B** and **D**; confusing since the other parts do not have a pause in these bars.

Bars 46-9, Oboes: 'col flauti a due' in **A**. **B** takes this to mean legato as flute as well as the same notes while **C** keeps the staccato of the previous bars. Note that in bar 71, the oboes are marked 'col flauti legato'.

Bar 51: *con molto forza* only for cellos in **B**, **D**; it was added in pencil at the bottom of the page in **A** and is given to viola, cello and bass in **C**.

Bar 77: Both cor anglais and chorus basses have a bar's rest in **D**. For the cor anglais, **A** has quaver b′ and rests, though no tie from previous bar, followed by **B** and **C**, both adding the tie. For the basses Dvořák added a quaver E and rests in pencil to **A**, matching cor anglais, clarinet and horn; **B** and **C** have taken the minim tied to quaver and rests given in **E**.

Bar 168: Dvořák added this note in **D**: 'NB Ringing of large and small bells to the sign (bar 182)'.

Bars 195-6: the voices are sustained to the first crotchet of 196 in **A**, matching trombone, tuba and timpani; **B** and **E** end on first crotchet of bar 195, as does **C** without comment. The longer note seems more logical.

Bars 198-200: **C** gives a timpani roll on e♭ through all three bars. It does not appear in **A** or **B**. Though present in the original version of **D** it was deleted in revision. However, Dvořák made a note in **D**, in ink, at the end of the movement: 'Timpani (copy into the printed score! / end) this number'. It is possible it should end at the first beat of bar 200, like the other instruments.

V

Bar 58: In his revision of **D**, Dvořák added **Un pochettino più mosso**. This is not given in **A**, but **Poco più mosso** has been added in blue, taken from **E**, '(non tanto)' is added in pencil.

Bar 85: No tempo mark in **A** or **D**; the **Meno, Tempo I** comes from **E**, and was added to **A** in blue. Since the mark at bar 58 was an afterthought of the composer's, he may well have overlooked the need for a return to the original tempo here.

VI

Tempo marks vary.

Bar 1: **D** has **Andante** for woodwind, **Andante ma non tanto** for soloists, and **Andante ma non troppo** for strings! **A** and **F** have **Andante ma non troppo**. **B**, **C**, **D** and **E** have **Andante**.

Bar 41: **A** and **D** have nothing. **B**, **E** and **F** have crotchet = 63, **C** has crotchet = 63 but puts it at bar 40.

Bar 53: **A** and **D** have nothing. **B**, **C**, and **E** have **Un pochettino più mosso**, crotchet = 66; **F** has the same but without MM.

Bar 64: **B**, **C** and **E** have **Tempo I**, crotchet = 60; **F** has **Tempo I** but no MM; **A** has the same added in blue. **C** makes no comment about **D**. It seems possible that all these tempo changes derive from **E**, and that Dvořák decided they were unnecessary in his final version.

Bar 80: The **a tempo** only appears in **C** and **E**, but is clearly needed after the *stringendo* at bar 76.

Other notes to movement VI

Bars 41-3. The dynamics for the soloists are confused. **A** and **D** have *m.v.* for bass entry, nothing for tenor entry, and in bar 43 soprano, alto and tenor are all marked *f*. In **E**, however, all entries are marked *mf mezza voce*, followed by **B** and **C**. Noting the accompanying dynamics this is probably correct.

Bar 60, Horn 3: Dotted minim in **A** and **D**, minim and crotchet rest in **B** and **C**, and a minim c′ in **E**. The clarinets also had a dotted minim in the original version, but Dvořák then changed this to minim and crotchet rest. **B** and **C** presumably consider Dvořák forgot to change the horn to match the clarinets. At the beginning of the stave in **D** there is a note: 'Horn has a mistake in the copy of the score'. This may refer to bar 60, but is perhaps more likely to refer to bar 62, a blank bar for the horn in **A**, with the tie from the previous bar deleted in pencil. Both note and tie are given in **B** and **C** (without comment).

Bar 88, Violin 1 note 1: The somewhat strange f′♯ is given in **A**, **B**, **D** and **E**, though in **B** it has been altered to d′ in ink, followed by **C**. Is it possible f′ double sharp was intended?

Bars 119-120, Alto, Tenor and Bass: quite different notes in **B** and **E**, further evidence that the engraver of **B** made much use of **E**, ignoring revisions by the composer.

Bar 122, Soprano: This edition and **C** follow the revised version in **D** and the autograph vocal score. **B** follows **E**, perhaps because the version in **A** makes no sense, appearing to be a confused conflation of the old and revised versions. Note also that bar 125 Bass beat 3 and bar 127 Tenor beat 1 had two quavers in **E**, again followed by **B** in spite of the clear notation of dotted quaver semiquaver in **A**.

VII

Bars 1-14, Trombones and tuba: **A** has *mf* in all bars except 6, which has *fz*! **C** gives editorial *fz* throughout. **C** also omits the *fz*s on beat 3 of violins in bars 1-4, clearly shown in **A**, giving instead the staccato dots used thereafter for the whole passage.

Bars 7, 8, Violins: Though the flats to d″ and g″ only appear in **E** they make good harmonic sense (note d′♭ for soloist and g♭ for cello and bass). Surprisingly **C** makes no comment.

Bar 102, Violin 1: **A** omits note 5 (b′); **B** does so too, solving the rhythmic problem by making all six notes quavers. Given as printed in **C**, **D** and **E**.

IX

The instructions concerning the use of mutes by the strings are thoroughly confusing in this movement.

Bar 32: **A** has *con sord.* for violins 1 and 2, but *senza sord.* for viola; *con sord.* has been added in ink to the cellos. **D** has *senza sord.* for the violas but nothing for the cellos. **C** has *con sord.* for all four parts.

Bar 73: **C** notes that **D** originally had *con sord.* here for violin 1 and cello, and for violin 2 at bar 83, but that in revision *senza sord.* was given instead. Though **C** also states that **B** has the *con sord.* for the three instruments it in fact has nothing, and nor does **A**.

Bar 77: **C** gives *senza sord.* in brackets to viola without further comment, **A** and **B** have nothing.

Bar 136: **B** has *senza sord.* for violins and violas, and added in ink to cellos; **A** and **C** have nothing. It seems improbable that Dvořák really intended the passage from bar 56-63, *f* triple stops for violins and *marcato* triplets *ff* for viola and cello, to be played with mutes. Though **A** has *con sord.* at bar 32 for three of the parts it

does not have *senza sord.* anywhere later in the movement! Perhaps mutes should be used from bars 32-41 only. Another possibility is that the *senza sord.* for viola given in **D** and confirmed by **A** was intended for the violins, who ended the previous movement with mutes. In this case mutes would not be used at all in this movement.

Bars 270-328, Timpani: **A** and **D** have upper f throughout, though in **A** bars 270 and 272 have this changed to low F in blue, followed by **B**. **C** gives low F throughout. There is no difficulty about using both Fs - after bar 148, B♭ can be changed to c and c to f.

X

Bars 54-6, Chorus basses: **B**, **C** and **E** give the notes shown in here in small print, though they disagree over dynamics; **B** follows **E** with nothing, *f* and *pp* for the three bars; **C** has *mf*, *f cresc.* hairpin and *pp*; while **F** has *mf*, *cresc.* hairpin and nothing! **D** has bar 56 empty, as does **A**, which also has the notes in bars 54 and 55 deleted in pencil. Probably Dvořák finally decided to leave the basses out here, leaving the horns alone as in bars 32-35.

XII

Dvořák revised this movement after the first performance to make things easier for the chorus. He had the altos double the first tenors almost throughout, instead of merely joining in from bar 97 to the end of the movement. At bar 16 he added a note in **D**: 'Should the choir sing flat, as happened at the first performance in Birmingham, it will be advisable for one horn to take over the note d′ from the first tenors, and sustain it into the following bar'.

Bars 24-32: 'At this place, too, support can be given by trombones – or (organ).' In **D** he wrote out parts for the three trombones, but in **A** the organ part is written in pencil and the trombone parts are omitted. All the other changes are added in pencil to **A** and accepted in **B**. With a capable choir perhaps these safety precautions could be ignored.

XIII

Bars 76-7: **C** states that the rhythm shown in the footnotes is given in **D** and in the first version of the autograph vocal score; in the vocal score it was altered to the main text, but this change was not copied into **D**, and so not **A** either.

Michael Pilkington
Old Coulsdon, 2001

1   Editor's Notes in Complete Works Full Score, Supraphon 1961.

REQUIEM MASS
PART I

ANTONÍN DVOŘÁK

No. 1   *Soli and Chorus* REQUIEM ÆTERNAM

2

4

* Bass: small notes missing in **A**

* Alto notes 3,4: e" c" in **A**   † Bars 105-8, Tenor: small notes in **A**, **D**

10

*Alto: as bar 131 in **A**, **D**, **F**; but see Sopranos bars 133,134, followed by **B**, **C**, **E**

* see Preface

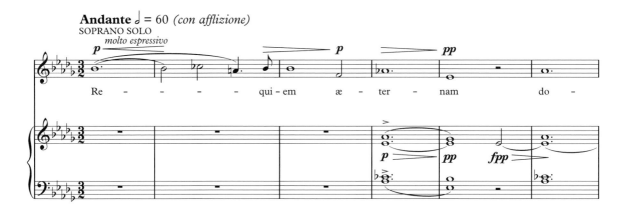

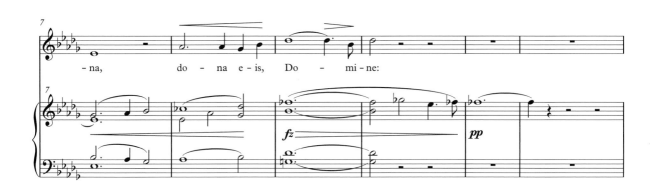

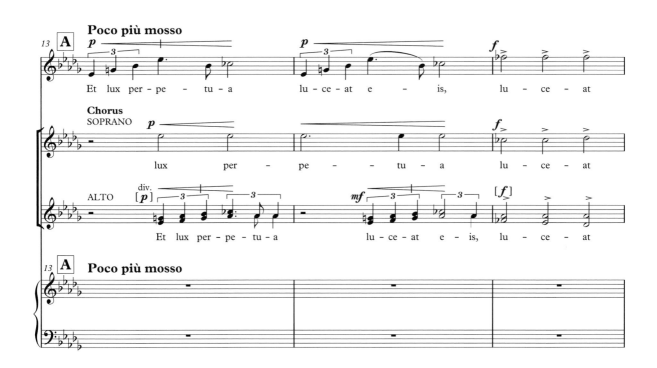

* 'rit' at beat three, **B, C, E**   † see Preface

* Bars 66,67, LH: see Preface   † Soprano note 2: a' in **A, B**; b' in **C, D, E**

18

* Tenor 1: natural missing in **A, B, D**

Chorus DIES IRÆ

24

Soli and Chorus TUBA MIRUM

et na-tu – ra.

pp

Mors stu-pe – bit et na-tu – –

– ra.

pp

ppp   *fz*   *pp*   *ppp*

★ RH notes, 7,10: f′ in **A**, **B**, **F**; e′ in **C**, **D**, **E**
† BASSES: ♩ ♪ ↟ ↟ in **B**, **C**, **E**; see Preface

Poco meno mosso

* MM ♩ = 69 in all sources, including **C**, but clearly an error, see Dies Irae

36

L'istesso tempo

* Small notes in **B, C, E,** only   † Tenors and Basses bar 195: ♩ ♩ ♩ − in **B, C, E;** see Preface

No. 5   *Soli and Chorus* QUID SUM MISER

* Soprano beat 4: ♪ (sic) in **D**; ♪ ⅞ in **A**; but see bars 27, 30

(Chorus)

(ALTO)

tunc dic - tu - - rus?

Quem pa - tro - num ro - ga - tu - rus, Cum vix

Quem pa - tro - num ro - ga - tu - rus, Cum vix

jus - tus sit se - cu - rus, cum vix jus - tus sit se - cu - rus?

jus - tus sit se - cu - rus, cum vix jus - tus sit se - cu - rus?

SOPRANO SOLO

Rex tre -

* Tenor Solo note 2: d' in **A** and **B**, e' in **C**, **D**, **E**

50

52

* see Preface

Quartet, RECORDARE, JESU PIE

* see Preface

* Basses beat 3, rhythm: ♩♪ **A**

* see Preface

* see Preface

59

* see Preface   † RH note 1: see Preface

* Soprano note 2: a'♭ in **A**; g' in **B**, **E**, **F**; b'♭ in **C**, **D**

* Soprano beat 3: ⌐ 3 ⌐ in **A**(!), ⌐ in **B, E, D** original version; see Preface

No. 7   *Chorus* CONFUTATIS MALEDICTIS

* Bars 7,8, RH: no flats to d" or g" in **A**, **B**, **C** (without comment), but given in **E**, see Preface

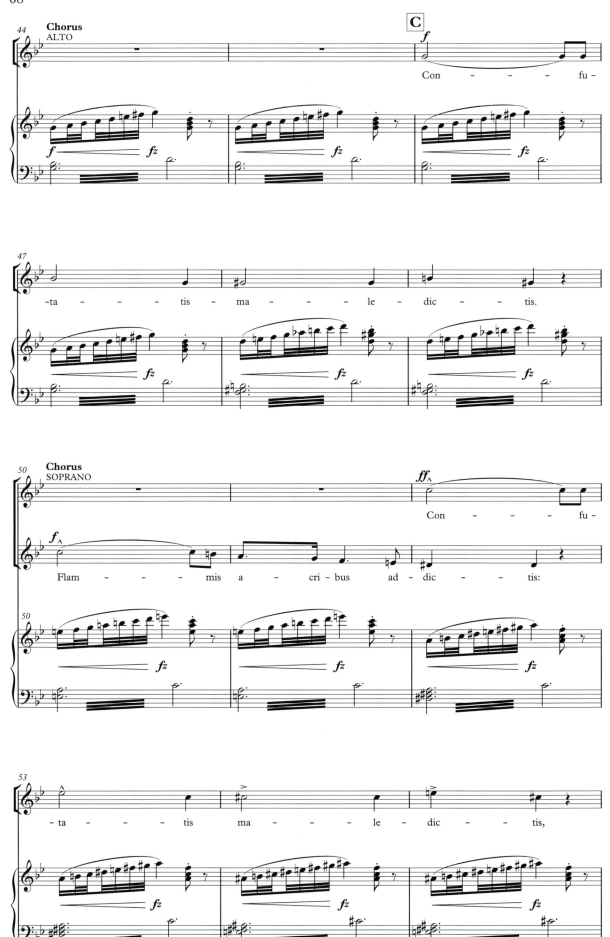

* Soprano note 1: e" sharp in **A, B**   † Soprano ♩ ♪ 𝄾 in **D**(sic), ♩ ♪ ♪ 𝄾 **A, F**   ** all voices: no dynamic **A, D; *ppp* B, C, E**

* Bars 88,90,92, Bass rhythm: ♩ ♩ in **B, C, E**

No. 8   *Soli and Chorus* LACRIMOSA

* Alto Solo bar 35 (and Soprano bar 71): 'parce' in all sources, but in error for 'ergo'?

* Alto solo: 'molto espressivo' in **C,E**   † Alto solo beats 2-3: ♩ ♪ in **E**

* Soloists: ♩ ♪ ♩ in **A, F**   † Alto and tenor soloists: ♩ ♪ ♫ in **B, C, E.**

* Bass: a, **A**, corrected to g in pencil; a, **B**

- - - men.

- - - men.

- - - men.

div.

- - - men.

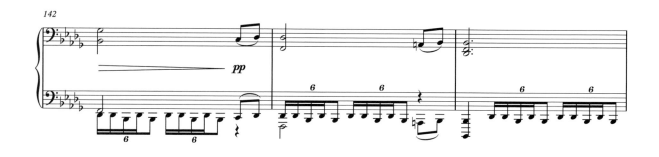

END OF PART 1

PART II

Soli and Chorus OFFERTORIUM

* Tenor and Bass; *f*, **B, C, E**

* Soprano and Alto: **mf**, **D**, **F**: **f** in pencil, **A**; **f**, **B**, **C**

90

★ Altos: *f*, **A**

98

* Alto notes 2-4: g' f' e' in **A, B**

* Tenor and Bass underlay: pro - mi -   **B, E, F,**

* Basses note 4: e♮, **A, D**

* Bass underlay: o - - - - - - - lim, quam in **B, E, C** (without comment); **A** has printed version added in pencil

* Bass under lay: - - jus. Quam o - lim in **B, C, E**

* Alto: f ' on first beat in **B, E** only; a' on fourth beat in **B, E** and **F**(!)

FINE

No. 10   *Soli and Chorus* HOSTIAS

★ LH note 3: c in **A, B, C** (without comment); but A in **E** and see bars 39, 82 and 112   † Alto: **A** and **D** have no dynamic; **B, C, E** have *f*

114

* Bass underlay: mor - te ___ in **B, E, F**

* Tenor 1 note 1: c' in **A**.   † Tenor 2 note 3: b in **A, B, D, E, F,** but see bars 60, 68 and 139; altered to a in **C**

Dal Segno (p.98) al Fine (p.110)

No. 11 *Soli and Chorus* SANCTUS

* "A small chorus", **B**, **C**, **E**; not in **A** or **D**

120

* Tenor underlay: cæ - li - et - in **A**

*all voices *f*, **A**

*Alto: in **B, E**

* Alto note 2: lower note omitted, **A, D**

No. 12

Soli and Chorus PIE JESU★

★ see Preface

* see Preface

* see Preface

No. 13

Soli and Chorus AGNUS DEI

144

* Soprano and Alto Chorus: ♩ ♪ ♩. ♪♪♩.♪♪♩.♪ in **A, D;** as printed, **B, C, E,** see bars 72,73, and Preface

150

* Soprano underlay: Do - mi - ne in **B, E,** without dynamics